CHARLES SELIGER

CHAOS TO COMPLEXITY

MARCH 13 – MAY 3, 2003

MICHAEL ROSENFELD GALLERY

NEW YORK

Among the most widely held views of Abstract Expressionism is the notion that it can be divided into two tendencies, the gestural and the geometric. A number of conclusions have been drawn with this viewpoint in mind, a key one being that in his poured paintings, Jackson Pollock was able to go beyond gesture, thus bringing about its demise. One effect of this notion is that the kind of expressionist brushwork we associate with someone like Willem de Kooning has never again been held in high regard. Another conclusion is that, in the decade following Pollock's death in 1956, the geometric ascended while the gestural devolved. Barnett Newman and Ad Reinhardt paved the way for Frank Stella and Minimalism, while, at best, de Kooning led to "second generation Abstract Expressionists" such as Norman Bluhm and Joan Mitchell. Among the numerous subtexts lurking within this narrow narrative is the assumption that Stella was able to create wholly American (and therefore truly new) art, while Bluhm and Mitchell were unable to sever their ties to European-inspired gestural painting, particularly as exemplified by de Kooning. Like a fairy tale with a predictable, happy ending, this view makes history and its subsequent unfolding neat and orderly, but it hardly addresses the real and far more complex story. A crucial component of that other history is the work of Charles Seliger, a truly unique American phenomenon.

In order to begin to recognize the importance of Seliger's achievements and their relevance to current modes of abstraction, it is necessary to mention a few salient details of his life. He was born in New York in 1926, and thus chronologically, he belongs to the same generation as Michael Goldberg (born 1926) and Helen Frankenthaler (born 1928). However, what isolates him from his own generation and connects him instead to the Abstract Expressionists (who are at least a decade older) is that Seliger exhibited his work in 1943 at the Norlyst Gallery; since then, he has continued to exhibit regularly in the United States and Europe. In 1943, he began experimenting with automatism, and it has remained an integral part of his process. In 1945, he had his first solo show at Peggy Guggenheim's Art of This Century gallery. In 1947, when Guggenheim closed her gallery and moved to Venice, Italy, she donated three paintings—two by Seliger and one by Jackson Pollock—to the permanent collection of the University of Iowa.

During these years, the precocious, self-taught teenager met many prominent and emerging figures, including André Breton, Marcel Duchamp, Max and Jimmy Ernst, Adolph Gottlieb, Gerome Kamrowski, Robert Motherwell, and Pollock. Seliger's friends and acquaintances constitute a who's who of the international art world. In hindsight, it seems remarkable that Seliger was never overwhelmed by the circle of brilliant older artists to which he belonged. Despite the heady artistic and literary milieu in which he moved, he was able to establish and pursue his own direction, which he continued to do for over six decades.

Seliger was able to maintain his own vision in the midst of those around him because he is a classic autodidact. Like two other notable autodidacts, Jasper Johns and Robert Ryman, Seliger did what most artists find impossible—he invented his own occasion. Johns has said he wanted to discover "what was helpless in my behavior." Ryman's education, which took place in the Museum of Modern Art (New York), where he worked for seven years, was propelled by his desire to "find out how things worked." In 1940, at the age of fourteen, Seliger began frequenting New York galleries and museums; it is during this time that he began to visit Julien Levy Gallery, Pierre Matisse Gallery and other galleries that showed work by the Surrealists. In 1945, when he was nineteen, he stated: "I want to apostrophize micro-reality. I want to tear the skin from life, and, peering closely, paint what I see. I want my brain to become a magnifying glass for the infinite minutiae forming reality. Growth is the poetry of all art." As their statements reveal, each of these artists found his own way into art, developing not only his own technique but also a visual language through which his vision could be expressed and understood.

Consistently a devoted student, Seliger possesses a singular inquisitiveness, a bottomless patience, and a need to be absolutely precise, character traits that observers have long recognized as being central to both Johns and Ryman. The connection between them goes deeper than their autodidacticism. For one thing, like Johns and Ryman, Seliger is neither an eccentric figure nor someone who has managed to carve a unique, but somewhat isolated niche for himself. In fact, the opposite is true. He is an important part of the mix, and his work embodies a centrality that has yet to be fully acknowledged.

In recent years, Seliger's centrality has become more obvious; he has presaged a number of routes currently being explored by both younger and established artists. His syncretic painting expands our understanding of modernism's capabilities. By drawing on a wide array of disparate sources, ranging from botany and physics to Mughal miniatures and Islamic calligraphy, he offers a useful alternative to modernism's reductive tendencies. Instead of regarding his work as an anomaly, an incredibly beautiful cul-de-sac in the history of painting, we should recognize to what extent Seliger has contributed to a vibrantly fertile current of artistic possibility running from recent history (modernism) to the unfolding present (postmodernism) and, we may imagine, well beyond.

There are many reasons for Seliger's marginalization within the standard history of Abstract Expressionism, the most obvious being scale. When we think of Abstract Expressionism, we think of large-scaled paintings, or what Clement Greenberg termed the "polyphonic" picture, which he believed provoked "the crisis of the easel picture." From the beginning of his career, Seliger has preferred to work on a small scale. His paintings from the 1940s are small, even by Surrealist standards, often measuring less than twenty-four inches by eighteen inches. His paintings since the early 1950s, when he came into his own, are neither easel pictures nor miniatures. Rather, they are something altogether unique: a highly detailed vision of both the infinite and the subatomic. However, because we so often understand gesture as writ large, we fail to recognize that within the small format he has chosen, Seliger also explores gesture. After all, isn't gesture a combination of matter and energy? Seliger is not interested in gestural action, but in the unseen phenomenon that constitute nature's gestures, from the Big Bang to the botanical. He comes to gesture from a different perspective, as a visionary observer rather than as a heroic practitioner.

In the current exhibition, *Chaos to Complexity*, the largest painting measures ten by eighteen inches, and the smallest one seven by five inches. While it is understandable to see Seliger's scale as proof of his modesty, it is a mistake to do so. It is also a mistake to believe that his preference for working on a small scale makes him derivative of Paul Klee, an acknowledged master of the diminutive. For one thing, Klee was not interested in either spatiality or the unity of the picture plane, which is to say he had only a passing interest in pure abstraction. Because Seliger's lines and dots are essentially abstract, and never function in a didactic way, his linearity differs significantly from Klee's. In Seliger's best paintings, the delicate tracery and meandering dots hover between description and pure color, which Klee's work does not do. In many of the paintings, the dots and tracery seem poised and ready to detach themselves from the material world.

In their myriad details, opulent opticality, translucency, layering, delicacy and compression, Seliger's paintings are unrivaled, and the artist's dazzling embrace of color only further elevates these paintings into a realm all their own. To begin to appreciate Seliger's mastery of color, imagine trying to tally and name each color, tone and hue inhabiting even a handful of his paintings.

Seliger's process consists of increasingly precise definitions and repeated articulation. Beginning with no specific idea in mind, the artist usually applies layers of acrylic paint to a Masonite surface. He may use a brush or a palette knife, and he will eventually sand or scrape through the many layers to "release images" that would have otherwise remained hidden in the paint. Seliger then begins to delineate the particular forms and coloristic shifts the paint yields. The initial delineations lead to further delineations. Through it all, Seliger is intimately aware of the presence of certain forms, and he lets them surface, sometimes following them, sometimes nudging them out to their imaginative conclusion. Looking at the results, we can imagine that Seliger moves from fine to finer brushes, until all he can use to apply the paint is a brush with a single hair. The result of this process is a surface that has been considered and reconsidered countless times. Everywhere one looks has been marked, gone over, examined.

One of the distinctive features of Seliger's obsessiveness is the feeling of immense patience that is clearly a guiding principle. Nothing in his work feels hurried, forced or done out of habit. Seliger's synthesis of obsessiveness, patience and calm with a sense of urgency is just one of the many visual paradoxes one encounters in these paintings. Moreover, Seliger's process is tremendously flexible and reveals a mastery of variety. In *Tranquility* (2002) (p.20), for example, many different layers of translucent color appear to have been compressed, while *Thaw* (2000) (p.6), tonally registers both large and small seismic shifts.

Seliger has transformed an immense and seemingly incommensurable range of sources, loves, and knowledge into his unmistakable mode of expression. And if this is not enough to stop us in our tracks, then consider the fact that each painting stands completely unique in its relationship to the others. Seliger does not repeat himself. He starts each painting fresh, and through his complete attentiveness, he arrives at something totally distinct. Seliger's paintings do nothing less than define their own necessity.

This distinctive singularity of Seliger's work stems in part from his mesmerizing sure-handed synthesis of tiny marks and numerous colors. There is not a whiff of nostalgia or sentimentality in his work. He shares very little with Joseph Cornell, another self-taught American who schooled himself on Surrealism. If anything, Seliger endows his paintings with a clear-eyed, forward-looking vision that celebrates our inevitable return to pure matter. For example, *Splendor* (2001) (cover), evokes a sense of glimpsing the cross section of dozens of crushed stones and gems packed tightly together, the universe shortly after the Big Bang, a picture of dark matter moving across time and space, a light-sensitive view of a subatomic world, dozens of different pigments suspended in

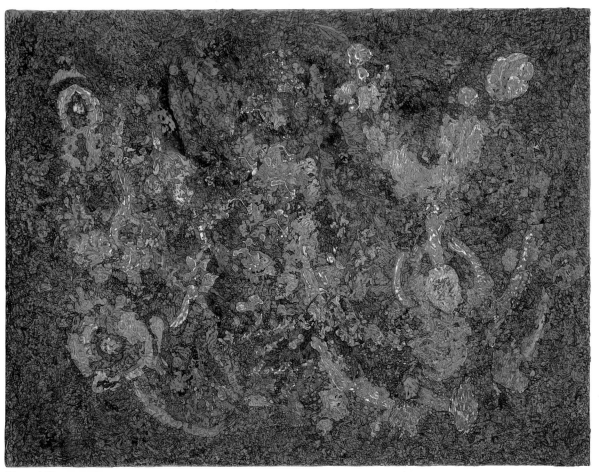

Natural History, 2002

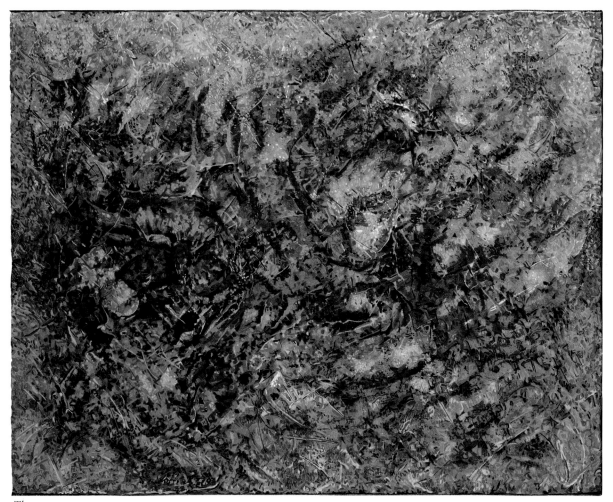

Thaw, 2000

a translucent material, rivulets of calligraphically inflected color swirling slowly. Time has been slowed down. *Splendor* is about as far removed from monochrome and geometry as one can imagine. The world it embodies consists of particles coalescing into gestures and gestures breaking up into particles. One is further struck by the fact that *Splendor* can be seen as developing out of either spiritual or scientific concerns. Despite their incommensurability, each perspective feels absolutely right.

Seliger's paintings may evoke botany, astronomy, mineralogy and particle physics, but ultimately they exist beyond any confining term we might try to apply to them. Like Pollock's poured paintings, they rigorously resist description and cannot be pinned down. In light of this observation, Seliger's undeniable achievement becomes clear: through the medium of paint, he has both constructed and investigated his own subject.

Seliger's hallucinatory work represent a largely neglected development in contemporary painting. By defining a process that integrates such disparate strands as his passionate interest in details, his deep commitment to automatism and chance, his unabashed love for the decorative and ornamental, his devotion to nature in all its manifestations and his belief that translucency and embellishment can fruitfully coexist, Seliger achieves a very different kind of painting than that of his early contemporaries, such as Pollock, Barnett Newman, Ad Reinhardt, or Mark Rothko. Rather than aligning himself with modernism's reductivist tendency, Seliger transforms tropes that many modernist practitioners and theoreticians pronounced both extraneous and unnecessary. It is not just that he has stubbornly gone against the grain, but that he uses modernist means like automatism to arrive at what has been deemed impossible to accomplish, a syncretic vision. Thus, Seliger not only embraces a wide range of divergent traditions, but he also explores this fecund realm with characteristic thoroughness. Only a supremely confident autodidact could have pulled off such an unlikely and ultimately subversive synthesis.

In his use of lines, dots, optical density and translucent layers, Seliger complicates the paradigm that divides Abstract Expressionism into the geometric and the gestural. In terms of the gestural, both Pollock and Seliger work spontaneously. Each transformed automatism and gesture into his own idiom. Thus, with Pollock and Seliger in mind, one can divide the gestural into two opposing tendencies, the expansive and the compressed, the outward and the inward, the macrocosmic and microcosmic. In contrast to Pollock, who extended his gestures while defining paint as paint, Seliger expanded paint's allusive powers, while compressing his gestures into tiny abstract and calligraphic marks.

Pollock's paint is quick; it dances unimpeded across the picture plane. His fluid gestures evoke what lies beyond the painting's frame. Seliger's paint moves slowly, deliberately, like molten lava. His tiny calligraphic marks, dots and stuttering lines evoke the infinite complexity of all matter. It is as if matter itself is being examined for all of its components, each of which contains even more components. Infinity, we might remember, grows in two directions, towards the vast and towards the minute.

Both Seliger and Pollock embody a unique understanding of the changing relationship between the expansive and the compressed. Ultimately, this division would be meaningless were it not for the many significant artists from different generations that seem to have picked up on possibilities that Seliger has been exploring for much of his career. Thus, one is tempted to suggest that while modernism's reductive tendency always seems on the verge of having played itself out, its inclusive tendency continues to surface in unexpected ways. And while we have paid attention to, as well as theorized, the former trope, it seems that we have repeatedly overlooked and downplayed the latter.

Anyone who stops to consider the current scene will soon see numerous connections between Seliger and younger artists. These connections make it evident that Seliger has been both defining and exploring a rich vein of possibilities. In his commitment to working in a small format, he is the forerunner of artists as disparate as Mark Greenwold, Bill Jensen, Eva Lundsager, Thomas Nozkowski, and Richard Tuttle. His multilayered, optically rich compositions and their highly precise, overlapping skeins of elusive traceries and dots anticipate the paintings of Steve Charles and the drawings of Gina Ferrari, Simon Frost, John Morrison and Daniel Zellner. Like Seliger, these artists compose through the accretion of small, distinct marks. In his innovative transformation of the traditions within the decorative arts, in particular the *fin de siecle* stylization of nature and the calligraphy and design of Islamic art, Seliger anticipates Philip Taaffe. Both Seliger and Taaffe are syncretic artists in their attention to detail and sources. In his interest in visionary states and perceiving what lies beyond surfaces, he shares something with Fred Tomaselli and Bruce Conner. All three have produced work of hallucinatory intensity. Finally, in transforming certain principles of Surrealism into his own idiom, Seliger reminds us that Surrealism remains alive and vital, not just as a kind of art, but as a way of thinking and doing, of being in this world.

By associating Seliger with artists as different as Steve Charles, Philip Taaffe, Bruce Conner, and Fred Tomaselli, I am suggesting that we should understand Charles Seliger not simply as a historical figure, but as a vital contemporary artist whose vibrant work has significance for us now. He brings us news that stays news. It is time we see his work for what it is—a profoundly intense and beautiful hallucinatory splendor.

John Yau is a writer, critic and publisher of Black Square Edition. His most recent books include *Borrowed Love Poems* (Penguin, 2002) and *My Heart Is That Eternal Rose Tattoo* (Black Sparrow, 2001). In 2002, he received grants from the Peter S. Reed Foundation and the Foundation for Contemporary Performance Art, and was named a Chevalier in the Order of Arts and Letters by the French government. He is the Critic in Residence at the Mount Royal School of Art, Maryland Institute College of Art. He lives in New York.

CHAOS TO COMPLEXITY

I HAVE INTERPRETED THE CONCEPTS OF CHAOS AND COMPLEXITY AS A PERSONAL

AESTHETIC. CHAOS, IS MY FIRST IMPRESSION OF THE PAINT. I HAVE RANDOMLY

APPLIED VARIOUS COLORS OF PAINT TO A SURFACE, BECAUSE IN THAT INITIAL

STAGE OF MY WORK, THERE ARE NO EMERGING FORMS OR IMAGES. AS I CONTINUE TO

PAINT, I TRY TO ORGANIZE THE SURFACE TO REFLECT MY AWE OF THE COMPLEXITY

FOUND WITHIN THE INFINITESIMAL FORMS OF THE NATURAL WORLD.

— CHARLES SELIGER

Heritage, 2003

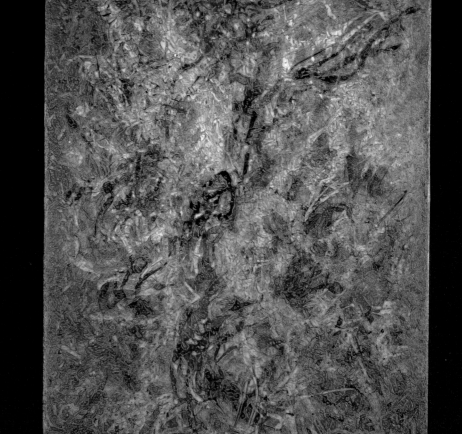

, 2002

Primal Blue, 2002

Crosscurrent, 2000

1 I, 2002

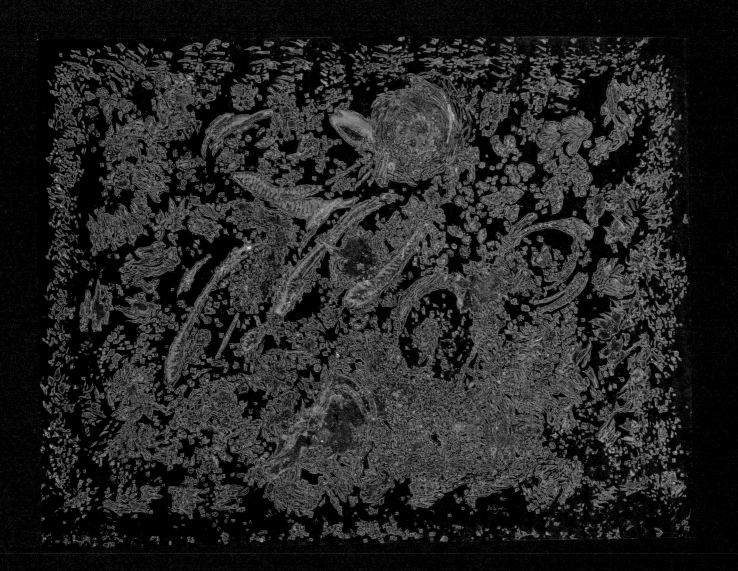

Constellation II, 2002

Crystal Garden, 2001

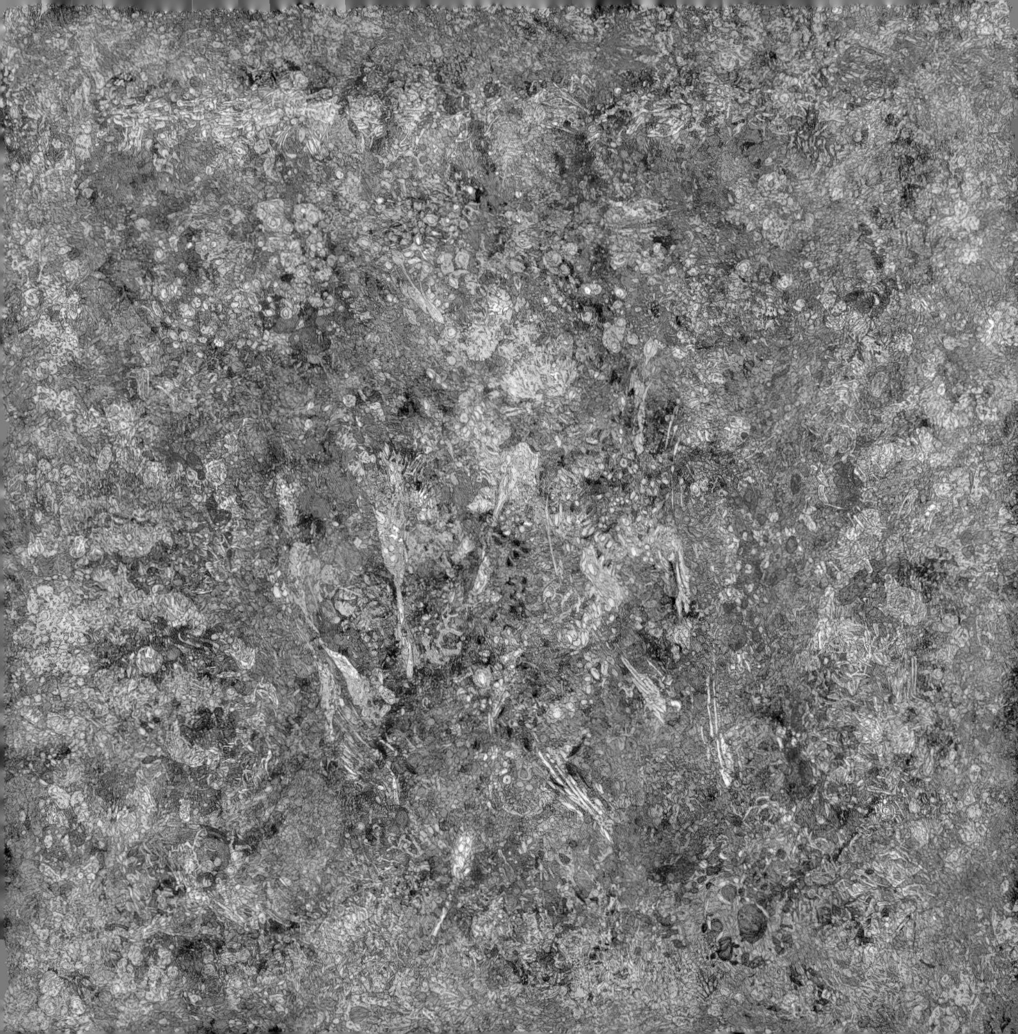

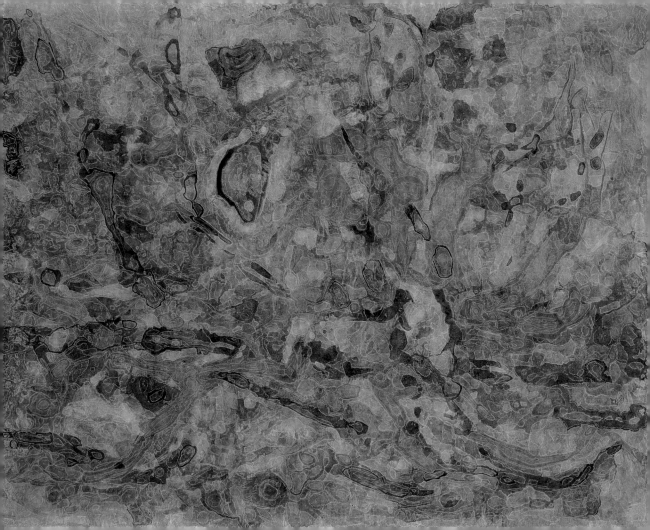

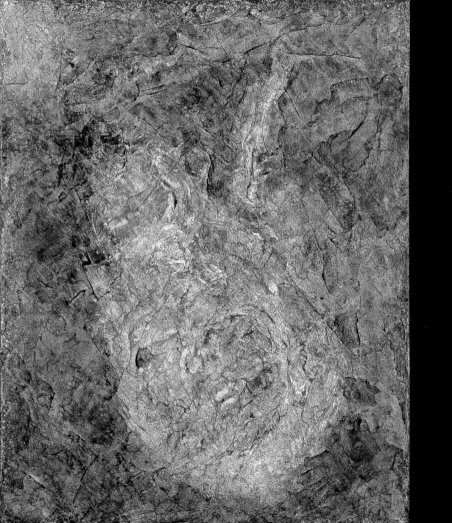

Sanctum, 2000

Spring Glory, 2002

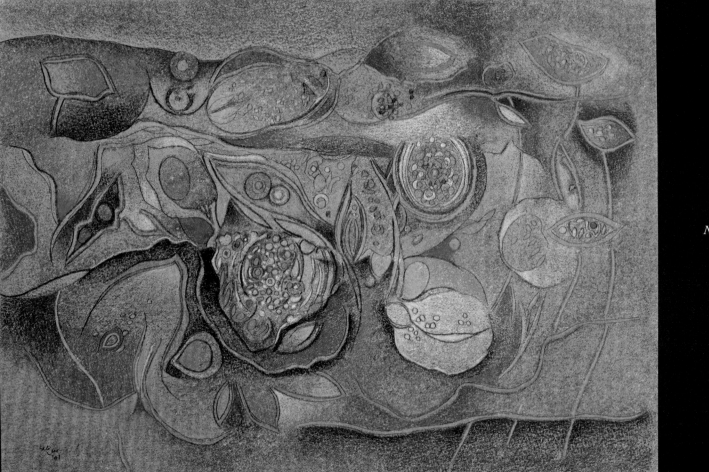

Nature's Way III, 2001

Sylvan Chamber, 2002

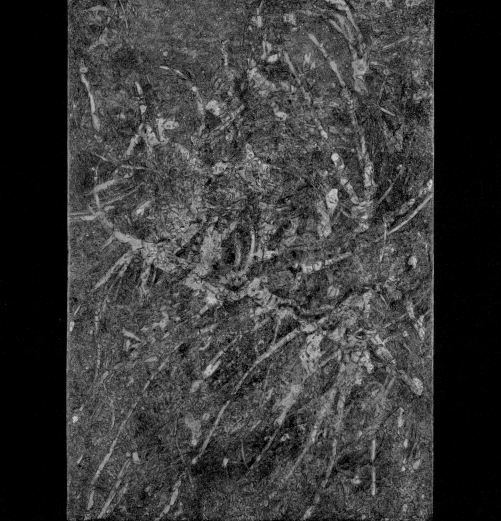

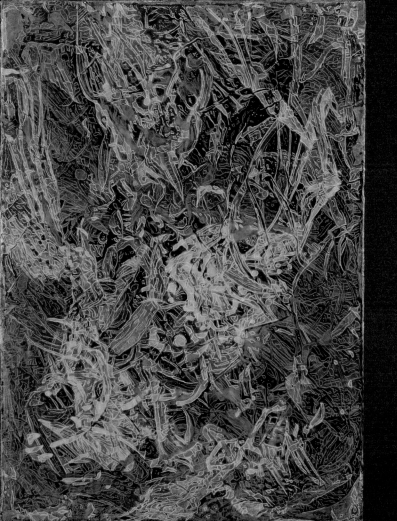

Convergence, 2002

Sunbright, 2001

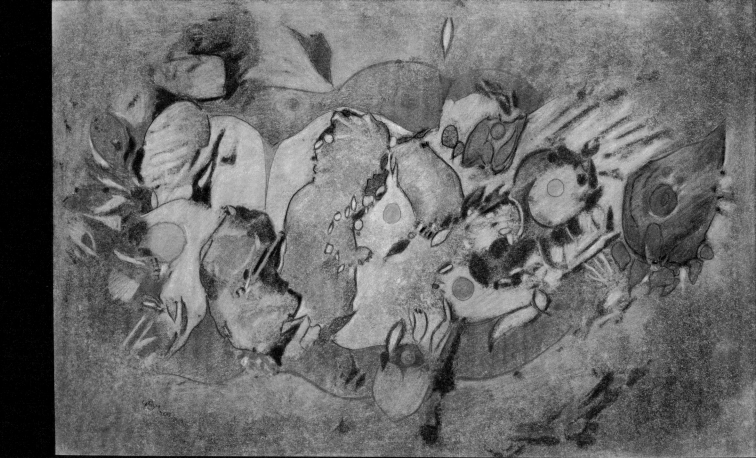

Excavation I, 2000

Excavation II, 2001

Autumn Rustlings, 2001

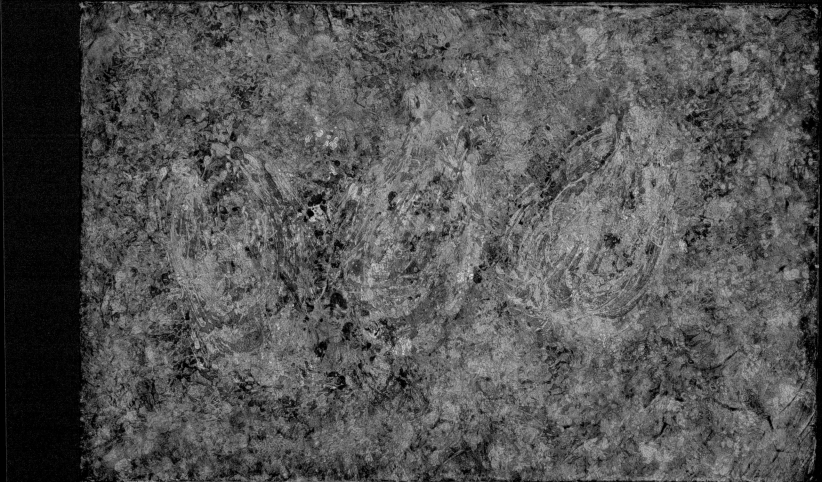

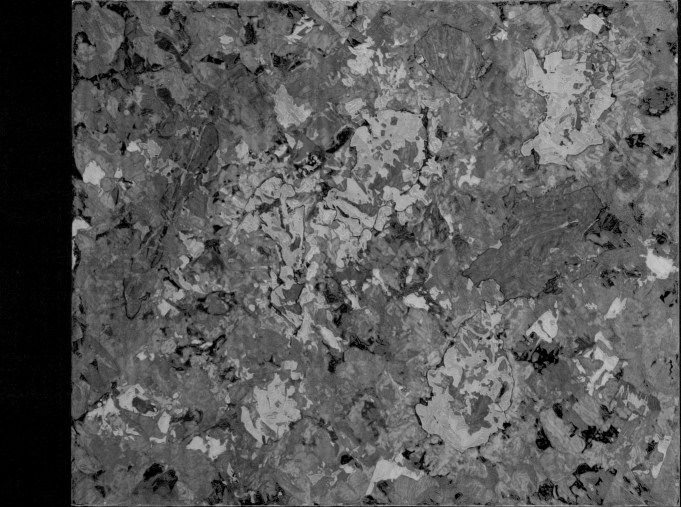

Stone Echoes, 2001

Mysterium, 2003

Crescendo, 2001

assage, 2002

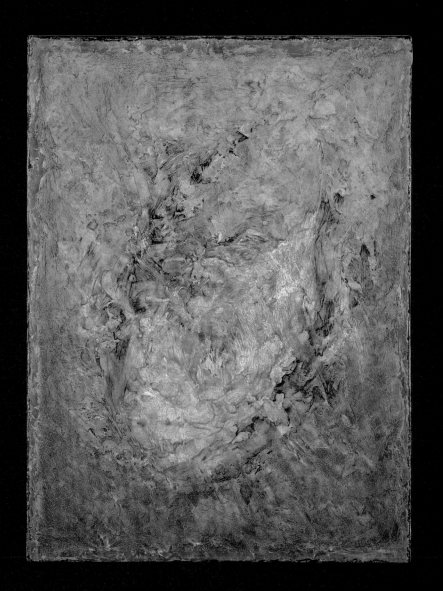

Nesting Place, 2000

Shattered Light, 2001

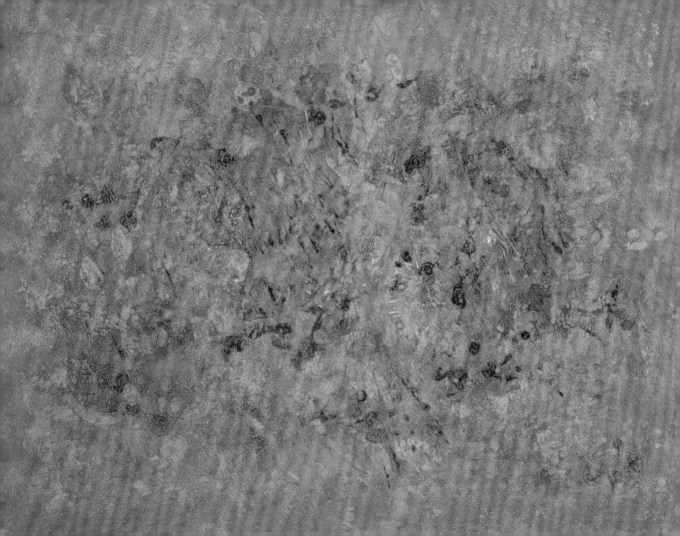

CHARLES SELIGER

SELECTED MUSEUM COLLECTIONS

Addison Gallery of American Art, Andover, MA
Arkansas Arts Center, Little Rock, AR
Art Institute of Chicago, Chicago, IL
Baltimore Museum of Art, Baltimore, MD
The British Museum, London, England
Brooklyn Museum of Art, Brooklyn, NY
Carnegie Museum of Art, Pittsburgh, PA
Fine Arts Museum of the South, Mobile, AL
Greenville County Museum of Art, Greenville, SC
High Museum of Art, Atlanta, GA
Hirshhorn Museum and Sculpture Garden, Washington, DC
The Israel Museum, Jerusalem, Israel
Jacksonville Art Museum, Jacksonville, FL
Jane Voorhees Zimmerli Art Museum, Rutgers University, New Brunswick, NJ
Long Beach Museum of Art, Long Beach, CA
The Metropolitan Museum of Art, New York, NY
Milwaukee Art Museum, Milwaukee, WI
Mississippi Museum of Art, Jackson, MS
Municipal Art Museum, The Hague, Holland
Munson-Williams-Proctor Institute, Utica, NY
Museum of Fine Arts, Houston, TX
Museum of Modern Art, New York, NY
Neuberger Museum of Art, Purchase College, State College of New York, Purchase, NY
The Newark Museum, Newark, NJ
New Orleans Museum of Art, New Orleans, LA
The New York Public Library, New York, NY
Ogunquit Museum of American Art, Ogunquit, ME
Peggy Guggenheim Collection, Venice, Italy
The Phillips Collection, Washington, DC
Rose Art Museum, Brandeis University, Waltham, MA
Seattle Art Museum, Seattle, WA
Solomon R. Guggenheim Museum, New York, NY
Staatliche Kunsthalle, Karlsruhe, Germany
Sunrise Art Museum, Charleston, WV
Wadsworth Atheneum Museum of Art, Hartford, CT
Whitney Museum of American Art, New York, NY
Worcester Art Museum, Worcester, MA

2003 Lee Krasner Lifetime Achievement Award given by the Pollock-Krasner Foundation

SOLO EXHIBITIONS

1945 Art of This Century gallery, New York, NY; 1946

1948 Carlebach Gallery, New York, NY; 1949

1949 M.H. de Young Memorial Museum, San Francisco, CA

Research Studio, Maitland, FL

Art Center School, Los Angeles, CA

1950 Willard Gallery, New York, NY; 1953, 54, 55, 57, 61, 62, 65-68

1955 Seligman Gallery, Seattle, WA; 1958, 65, 66

1966 Nassau Community College, Garden City, NY

1969 Wooster Community Art Center, Danbury, CT

1974 Andrew Crispo Gallery, New York, NY; 1976, 78, 79, 81, 83

1976 Les Copains Art Ltd., Buffalo, NY

1979 Makler Gallery, Philadelphia, PA

1981 Frances Wolfson Art Gallery, Miami-Dade Community College, Miami, FL

Jacksonville Art Museum, Jacksonville, FL

1985 Gallery Schlesinger-Boisante, New York, NY; 1986, 87

1986 Solomon R. Guggenheim Museum, New York, NY

Galerie Lopes, Zurich, Switzerland; 1989, 90

1990 Saidenberg Gallery, New York, NY

1991 *Charles Seliger: Undercurrents,* Michael Rosenfeld Gallery, New York, NY

1992 *Charles Seliger, Infinities, Recent Paintings,* Michael Rosenfeld Gallery, New York, NY

1994 *Charles Seliger, Natures Journal: Recent Paintings and Gouaches,* Michael Rosenfeld Gallery, New York, NY

1995 *Charles Seliger: The 1940s & 1990s,* Michael Rosenfeld Gallery, New York, NY

1997 *Charles Seliger, Biomorphic Drawings, 1944-1947,* Michael Rosenfeld Gallery, New York, NY

1999 *Charles Seliger, The Nascent Image, Recent Paintings,* Michael Rosenfeld Gallery, New York, NY

2003 *Charles Seliger, Chaos to Complexity,* Michael Rosenfeld Gallery, New York, NY

Charles Seliger: Sixty Years of Abstraction, Greenville County Museum of Art, Greenville, SC

SELECTED GROUP EXHIBITIONS

1943 *Adventures in Perspective,* Norlyst Gallery, New York, NY

40 American Moderns, 67 Gallery, New York, NY

1944 *Captured Light: Experimental Painting and Photography,* Norlyst Gallery, New York, NY

Painters and Sculptors Society of New Jersey, Jersey City Museum, Jersey City, NJ

1945 *A Painting Prophecy,* David Porter Gallery, Washington, DC; The Rochester Memorial Art Gallery, Rochester, NY

A Problem for Critics, 67 Gallery, New York, NY

Autumn Salon, Art of This Century gallery, New York, NY

1946 *Fifth Biennial, Contemporary American Paintings,* Virginia Museum of Fine Arts, Richmond, VA

Five Young Americans, Art of This Century gallery, New York, NY

Second Annual, Contemporary Art, The State University, Iowa City, IO

1947 *58th Annual Exhibition of American Abstract and Surrealist Art,* Art Institute of Chicago, Chicago, IL for The American Federation of Arts

Third Annual Contemporary Art, State University of Iowa, Iowa City, IA

1948 *Realities Nouvelles,* Salon des Realites Nouvelles, Paris, France

New American Painters, Museum of Modern Art, New York, NY

Annual Exhibition, Contemporary American Paintings, Whitney Museum of American Art, New York, NY; 1949, 51-58, 60

Recent Acquisitions, An Exhibition of Painting, Sculptures, Constructions and Drawings, Museum of Modern Art, New York, NY

1949 *24th Venice Biennial,* Peggy Guggenheim Collection, Venice, Italy

15th Biennial International Watercolor Exhibition, Brooklyn Museum of Art, Brooklyn, NY; 1951, 57, 59

1950 *American Painting 1950,* Virginia Museum of Fine Arts, Richmond, VA

American Painting and Sculpture, The Newark Museum, Newark, NJ

Spiral Group, Riverside Museum, New York, NY

Barnyard Zoo, Baltimore Museum of Art, Baltimore, MD

1951 *Abstract Painting and Sculpture in America,* Museum of Modern Art, New York, NY

Annual American Exhibition, Art Institute of Chicago, Chicago, IL; 1955, 61, 62, 64

Young Painters USA, Herbert F. Johnson Museum of Art, Cornell University, Ithaca, NY

1952 *Contemporary Drawings from Twelve Countries,* Art Institute of Chicago, Chicago, IL

Painter's Choice, Worcester Art Museum, Worcester, MA

Contemporary New Jersey Artists, The Newark Museum, Newark, NJ

Land, Sea and Air, Children's Museum of Denver Art Museum, Denver, CO

1953 *Abstract Painting in America,* Syracuse Museum of Fine Arts, Syracuse, NY

63rd Annual Exhibition, Nebraska Art Association, Lincoln, NB

1954 *American Painting 1954,* Virginia Museum of Fine Arts, Richmond, VA

American Painting 1954, Des Moines Art Center, Des Moines, IA

1955 *Contemporary American and European Paintings,* Columbus Museum of Fine Arts, Columbus, OH

Pittsburgh International, Carnegie Institute, Pittsburgh, PA

Contemporary American and European Paintings, John Herron Art Museum, Indianapolis, IN

1956 *Recent Accessions,* Wadsworth Atheneum, Hartford, CT

1957 *New York Artists 6th Annual Exhibition,* Stable Gallery, New York, NY

L'Arte Grafica Contemporanea, Stati Uniti, Gallerie Nazionale d'Arte Moderna, Rome, Italy

Twentieth Century American Graphic Arts, United States Information Agency (traveled)

Edward Wales Root, An American Collector, Munson-Williams-Proctor Institute, Utica, NY; Addison Gallery of American Art, Andover, MA, University of Michigan Museum of Art, Ann Arbor, MI

1958 *75th Annual Exhibition,* Portland Museum of Art, Portland, ME

The New Landscape in Art and Science, The American Federation of the Arts, New York, NY

3rd Annual Exhibition of Contemporary Painting, Dupont Galleries, Mary Washington College of the University of Virginia, Fredericksburg, VA

1959 *Contemporary American Watercolors,* John Herron Art Museum, Indianapolis, IN

National Drawing Competition, Boston Museum of Fine Arts, Boston, MA

4th Exhibition of Modern Art, Mary Washington College of the University of Virginia, Fredericksburg, VA

Selected Drawings from National Drawing Competition, Boston Museum of Fine Arts, DeCordova and Dana Museum, Lincoln, MA

1960 *The Importance of the Small Painting,* The Nordness Gallery, New York, NY

1961 *The Quest and the Quarry,* Rome-New York Art Foundation, Rome, Italy

Ninth Annual Exhibition, Ogunquit Museum of Art, Ogunquit, ME

Sixth Exhibition of Modern Art, Mary Washington College of the University of Virginia, Fredericksburg, VA

1962 *157th Annual Exhibition of American Painting and Sculpture,* Pennsylvania Academy of the Fine Arts, Philadelphia, PA

Edward R. Root Bequest, Munson-Williams-Proctor Institute, Utica, NY

Three Painters, Haydon Calhoun Galleries, Dallas, TX

New Accessions USA, Colorado Springs Fine Arts Center, Colorado Springs, CO

1963 *Art for American Embassies,* Department of State, Washington, DC

Contemporary Masters Drawings and Prints, Providence Art Club, Providence, RI

1964 *Watercolors and Drawings,* Munson-Williams-Proctor Institute, Utica, NY

1965 *Contemporary American Paintings and Sculpture,* University of Illinois, Urbana, IL

10th Exhibition of Modern Art, Mary Washington College of the University of Virginia, Fredericksburg, VA

1966 *Selections from the Permanent Collection,* Rose Art Museum, Brandeis University, Waltham, MA

Drawings USA '66, 3rd Biennial Exhibition, Saint Paul Art Center, MN

Childe Hassam and Eugene Speicher Purchase Fund Exhibition, American Academy of Arts and Letters, New York, NY

1967 *XXII American Drawing Biennial,* Norfolk Museum of Fine Arts and Sciences, Norfolk, VA

1968 *The Art of Organic Forms,* Smithsonian's Museum of Natural History, Washington, DC

Childe Hassam and Eugene Speicher Purchase Fund Exhibition, American Academy of Arts and Letters, New York, NY

1970 *Miniaturan '70 International,* Galerie 66 HG, Hofheim, West Germany

Art for Peace, Laguardia Place, New York, NY

1975 *20th Century American Painting and Sculpture,* Andrew Crispo Gallery, New York, NY

1976 *20th Century American Masters,* Andrew Crispo Gallery, New York, NY

Watercolors: Historical and Contemporary, Skidmore College, Saratoga Springs, NY

1977 *This Is Today: An Exhibition of Works by Living Artists,* Root Center, Hamilton College, Clinton, NY

Members' Gallery, Albright-Knox Art Gallery, Buffalo, NY

Recent Acquisitions, Solomon R. Guggenheim Museum, New York, NY

1979 *Works on Paper, USA,* Rockland Center for the Arts, West Nyack, NY

1981 *New York Gallery Showcase,* Oklahoma Art Center, Oklahoma, OK

Contemporary American Landscape, Taft Museum, Cincinnati, OH

Bouquet, Summit Art Center, Summit, NJ

1982 *Solitude, Inner Visions in American Art,* Terra Museum of American Art, Chicago, IL

Drawings by Picasso and Paul Klee, Abstractions by Charles Seliger, Saidenberg Gallery, New York, NY

The Spirit of Paper: 20th Century American, Frances Wolfson Art Gallery, Miami, FL

1987 *Peggy Guggenheim's Other Legacy,* Solomon R. Guggenheim Museum, New York and The Peggy Guggenheim Collection, Venice, Italy

Le Eredita Sconosciute Di Peggy Guggenheim, Collezione Peggy Guggenheim, Venice, Italy

Nature Into Art, Munson-Williams-Proctor Institute, Utica, NY

Watercolor Now, Frances Wolfson Art Gallery, Miami-Dade Community College, Miami, FL

Visions of Inner Space, Wright Art Gallery, UCLA, Los Angeles, CA; National Gallery of Modern Art, New Delhi, India

Inaugural Exhibition, Sid Deutsch Gallery, New York, NY

1989 *Abstract Expressionism, Other Dimensions,* Lowe Art Museum, Miami, FL; Terra Art Museum of American Art, Chicago, IL; Zimmerli Art Museum, New Brunswick, NJ; Whitney Museum of American Art at Philip Morris, New York, NY

Late 19th and 20th Century American Masters, Sid Deutsch Gallery, New York, NY

Art on Paper 1989, Weatherspoon Art Gallery, University of North Carolina, Greensboro, NC

Works on Paper, Sid Deutsch Gallery, New York, NY

1990 *Watercolors from the Abstract Expressionist Era,* Katonah Art Museum, Katonah, NY

An Artist's Christmas, Holiday Images of American Artists 1880-1990, Midtown Payson Galleries, New York, NY

Stamens and Pistils: Interpreting the Flower 1790-1990, Louis Stern Galleries, Beverly Hills, CA

1991 *Watercolor Across the Ages,* Bristol-Myers Squibb Gallery, Princeton, NJ

Nature's Rhythm, Snyder Fine Art, New York, NY

1992 *Kandinsky and the American Avant-Garde,* Terra Museum, Chicago, IL; The Phillips Collection, Washington, DC; Amon Carter Museum, Fort Worth, TX; Dayton Art Institute, Dayton, OH

1993 *Expressions,* Zimmerli Art Museum, Rutgers University, New Brunswick, NJ

Lines & Myths: Abstraction in American Art, 1941-51, Michael Rosenfeld Gallery, New York, NY

Aspects of American Abstraction, 1930-42, Michael Rosenfeld Gallery, New York, NY

1994 *On Paper: Abstraction in America,* Michael Rosenfeld Gallery, New York, NY

1995 *Collage: Made in America,* Michael Rosenfeld Gallery, New York, NY

Exploring the Unknown: Surrealism in American Art, Michael Rosenfeld Gallery, New York, NY

A Twentieth Century Survey of American Watercolor,

Southern Alleghenies Museum of Art, Loretto, PA

Surrealism in Exile, La Maison Francaise, New York University, New York, NY

1997 *Surrealism and American Art 1932-1949,* The Boca Raton Museum of Art, Boca Raton, FL

1998 *The Surrealist Vision: Europe and the Americas,* Bruce Museum, Greenwich, CT

Original Scale, Apex Art C.P., New York, NY

Essence of the Orb, Michael Rosenfeld Gallery, New York, NY

Peggy Guggenheim: A Centennial Celebration, Solomon R. Guggenheim Museum, New York, NY

1999 *Surrealism in America During the 1930s and 1940s: Selections from the Penny and Elton Yasuna Collection,* Salvador Dali Museum, St. Petersburg, FL

The Surrealists in Exile and the Origin of the New York School, Museo Nacional Centro de Arte Reina Sofia, Madrid, Spain; Musées de Strasbourg, Strasbourg, France

Severed Ear: The Poetry of Abstraction, The Creiger-Dane Gallery, Boston, MA

Paper Invitational II, Woodward Gallery, New York, NY

Linear Impulse, Michael Rosenfeld Gallery, New York, NY

Calm and Commotion: Abstract Art from the Permanent Collection, Mississippi Museum of Art, Jackson, MS

Impossible Landscapes of the Mind, Hirschl & Adler Galleries, New York, NY

2000 *Bug Out,* Munson-Williams-Proctor Arts Institute, Utica, NY

Michael Rosenfeld Gallery: The First Decade, Michael Rosenfeld Gallery, New York, NY

2001 *Jazz and Visual Improvisation,* Katonah Art Museum, Katonah, NY

Flora: In Reverence of Nature, Michael Rosenfeld Gallery, New York, NY

Paper Assets: Collecting Prints and Drawings, 1996-2000, The British Museum, London, England

Vital Forms: American Art and Design in the Atomic Age, 1940-1960, Brooklyn Museum of Art, Brooklyn, NY; Walker Art Center, Minneapolis, MN; Frist Center for the Visual Arts, Nashville, TN; Phoenix Art Museum, Phoenix, AZ

1950-65: Abstraction on Paper, Michael Rosenfeld Gallery, New York, NY

2002 *Transitions at Mid-Century, Works on Paper 1945-1955,* Whitney Museum of American Art, New York, NY

2003 *On Paper: Masterworks from the Addison Collection,* Addison Gallery of American Art, Andover, MA

The Art of Organic Forms, Michael Rosenfeld Gallery, New York, NY

Conversations: A Collection in Dialogue, Addison Gallery of American Art, Andover, MA

Michael Rosenfeld Gallery is the exclusive representative of Charles Seliger.

CHECKLIST OF THE EXHIBITION

CREDITS

Exhibition Coordinators
halley k harrisburg
Michael Rosenfeld

Catalogue Design and Editor
halley k harrisburg

Catalogue Essay
© John Yau

Editorial Assistant
Kim Driessen

Catalogue Photography
Joshua Nefsky

Catalogue Art Direction
and Production
CP Design

Catalogue Typeface
Tannhauser, Adobe Garamond

Catalogue Printing
Oceanic Graphic Printing, Inc.

Printed in China
Edition 1500
ISBN #1-930416-23-7

© Michael Rosenfeld Gallery
24 West 57 Street, 7th Floor
New York, NY 10019
(212) 247-0082
(212) 247-0402 fax

www.michaelrosenfeldart.com

Gallery Hours:
Tuesday through Saturday
10:00-6:00

ADAA member

Our gratitude for the insightful essay
provided by John Yau.

This exhibition coincides with the
release of the monograph *Charles Seliger:
Redefining Abstract Expressionism* by
Francis V. O'Connor, published by
Hudson Hills Press.

MICHAEL
ROSENFELD
GALLERY
PUBLICATIONS

A Selection of Twentieth Century American Art . . . . December 10, 1989 - March 25, 1990

Surrealism & Magic Realism in American Art . . . . .April 1–June 1, 1990

Raphael & Moses Soyer . . . . .June 4–July 20, 1990

Dwinell Grant: Drawings for "Contrathemis" . . . . .September 4–October 6, 1990

Figures of Speech: Social Realism of the WPA Era . . . . .October 9–November 17, 1990

Charles Seliger: Undercurrents . . . . .February 5–March 9, 1991

American Abstract Artists: 1930s & 1940s . . . . .March 14–April 27, 1991

Benjamin Benno: 1930s American Modernist in Paris . . . . May 4–June 15, 1991

Byron Browne: Evolution of an American Modernist, 1930s-1950s . . . . September 21–October 26, 1991

Pavel Tchelitchew: Nature Within & Without . . . . .October 31–December 14, 1991

Surrealism Embodied: The Figure in American Art, 1933-1953 . . . . February 13–March 28, 1992

Charles Seliger: Infinities, Recent Paintings . . . . .April 4–May 9, 1992

The WPA Era: Urban Views & Visions . . . . .May 12–June 27, 1992

Federico Castellon: Surrealist Paintings Rediscovered, 1933-1934 . . . . September 12–October 31, 1992

Lines & Myths: Abstraction in American Art, 1941-1951 . . . . November 5–January 20, 1993

Aspects of American Abstraction, 1930-1942 . . . . .February 11–March 27, 1993

Pavel Tchelitchew: Nature Transformed . . . . .April 3–May 29, 1993

On Paper: The Figure in 20th Century American Art . . . . June 10–August 15, 1993

Boris Margo: Surrealism to Abstraction, 1930-1952 traveled to Center for the Arts, Vero Beach, FL . . . . September 31- November 12, 1993

African-American Art: 20th Century Masterworks . . . . November 18–February 12, 1994

Charles Seliger: Nature's Journals, Recent Paintings and Gouaches . . . . February 19–April 2, 1994

Counterpoints: American Art, 1930-1945 . . . . .April 7–June 4, 1994

On Paper: Abstraction in American Art . . . . .June 9–August 12, 1994

Perceivable Realities: Eilshemius, Graves, Tanner and Tchelitchew . . . . September 22–November 10, 1994

Gallery II: Martha Madigan: Human Nature . . . . .September 22–November 10, 1994

Planes, Trains & Automobiles: Machine-Age America . . . . .November 17–January 22, 1995

Gallery II: Irene Rice Pereira: Monumental Paintings, 1932-1938 . . . . November 17–January 22, 1995

African-American Art: 20th Century Masterworks, II traveled to Long Beach Museum of Art, Long Beach, CA . . . . February 1–April 8, 1995

Burgoyne Diller: A Pioneer of Abstraction . . . . .April 13–June 3, 1995

Gallery II: Charles Seliger: The 1940s & 1990s . . . . April 13–June 3, 1995

Collage: Made in America . . . . .June 8–August 25, 1995

Gallery II: Fairfield Porter: Drawings and Poetry . . . . .June 8–August 25, 1995

William H. Johnson: Works from the Collection of Mary Beattie Brady . . . . September 14–November 11, 1995

Gallery II: Beauford Delaney: Paris Abstractions from the 1960s . . . . September 14–November 11, 1995

Exploring the Unknown: Surrealism in American Art . . . . November 16–January 27, 1996

Gallery II: Boris Margo: Fantasy in Form . . . . November 16–January 27, 1996

African-American Art: 20th Century Masterworks, III . . . . January 31–April 6, 1996

Clifford Odets: "In Hell + Why": Paintings 1940s & 1950s traveled to Oregon Shakespeare Festival, Ashland, OR
and Williams College Museum of Art, Williamstown, MA . . . . April 11–June 8, 1996

Alfonso Ossorio: The Creeks—Before, During and After at Ossorio Foundation, Southampton, NY . . . . .June 1–September 4, 2000

Charmion von Wiegand: Spirituality in Abstraction, 1945-1969 . . . . .September 7–October 28, 2000

Gallery II: Blanche Lazzell: American Modernist . . . . .September 7–October 28, 2000

Nancy Grossman: Loud Whispers traveled to The Greenville County Museum of Art, Greenville, SC;
Savannah College of Art and Design, Savannah, GA . . . . .November 2, 2000–January 13, 2001

Gallery II: Sensual Lines: American Figurative Drawings . . . . .November 2, 2000–January 13, 2001

African-American Art: 20th Century Masterworks, VIII traveled to
Texas Southern University Museum, Houston, TX . . . . .January 18–March 10, 2001

Out of the Fifties—Into the Sixties: 6 Figurative Expressionists . . . . .March 15–May 5, 2001

Martha Madigan: Vernal Equinox, Recent Photograms . . . . .May 9–June 30, 2001

Gallery II: Flora: In Reverence of Nature . . . . .May 9–June 30, 2001

Synergy: Alfonso Ossorio and Jackson Pollock, 1950-1951 at Ossorio Foundation, Southampton, NY . . . . .June 1–September 2, 2001

Alma Thomas: Phantasmagoria, Major Paintings traveled to The Women's Museum, Dallas, TX . . . . .September 13–November 3, 2001

Gallery II: Abstraction on Paper, 1950–1965 . . . . .September 13–November 3, 2001

Burgoyne Diller: The 1930s, Cubism to Abstraction . . . . .November 8, 2001–January 12, 2002

Gallery II: Theodoros Stamos: Allegories of Nature, Organic Abstractions traveled to Asheville Art Museum, Asheville, NC . . . . .November 8, 2001–January 12, 2002

African-American Art: 20th Century Masterworks, IX
traveled to Tubman African American Museum, Macon, GA . . . . .January 17–March 9, 2002

Jay DeFeo: Ingredients of Alchemy, Before and After The Rose . . . . .March 14–May 4, 2002

Alfonso Ossorio: Horror Vacui . . . . .May 9–July 29, 2002

Alfonso Ossorio: Horror Vacui at Ossorio Foundation, Southampton, NY . . . . .May 30–September 1, 2002

Gallery II: Clifford Odets: Paradise Lost, Paintings on Paper . . . . .May 9–July 29, 2002

Betye Saar: Colored—Consider the Rainbow traveling to The Columbus Museum Uptown, Columbus, GA . . . . .September 12–November 2, 2002

Louis Stone: American Modernist, Major Paintings 1930-1942 . . . . .November 7, 2002–January 11, 2003

Gallery II: Early American Abstraction: Small Scale—Large Dimension . . . . .November 7, 2002–January 11, 2003

African-American Art: 20th Century Masterworks, X . . . . .January 16–March 8, 2003

Charles Seliger: Chaos to Complexity . . . . .March 13–May 3, 2003

Gallery II: The Art of Organic Forms . . . . .March 13–May 3, 2003

American Identity: Figurative Painting and Sculpture, 1930–1945 . . . . .May 9–July 11, 2003

Gallery II: Ben Shahn: Freedom of Speech . . . . .May 9–July 11, 2003